THE QUEST FOR THE CRYSTAL

ADAPTED BY KATE HOWARD

■SCHOLASTIC

Scholastic Children's Books
Euston House,
24 Eversholt Street,
London NW1 1DB, UK

A division of Scholastic Ltd
London ~ New York ~ Toronto ~ Sydney ~ Auckland
Mexico City ~ New Delhi ~ Hong Kong

This book was first published in the US in 2016 by Scholastic Inc.
Published in the UK by Scholastic Ltd, 2016

ISBN 978 1407 16223 2

Printed in Italy

2 4 6 8 10 9 7 5 3 1

Papers used by Scholastic Children's Books are made from woods grown in sustainable forests.

www.scholastic.co.uk

A DANGEROUS QUEST

Cole, Jay, Kai and Zane were on a dangerous quest. They were racing to find the powerful Realm Crystal before Morro, the ghostly Master of Wind, could find it.

The ninja were also searching for Lloyd, whose form Morro had taken over. His friends hoped that if they found the crystal, they would also be able to rescue Lloyd.

The ninja were deep under the ocean in *Airship Rex*. The secret entrance to the Tomb of the First Spinjitzu Master was far below the water's surface. The Realm Crystal was hidden somewhere in the tomb.

Sensei Wu spoke to the ninja on their monitor. "Find the Realm Crystal before Morro does."

The ninja knew this would be difficult. They had lost their elemental powers when Morro escaped the Cursed Realm. Plus, they had to complete a series of challenges to reach the crystal.

Jay gulped. "Cole's a ghost, Kai can't swim, we have no magical sword, no elemental powers . . . What could go wrong?"

On-screen, Misako shared some words of advice. "I have discovered a riddle that may help you in the tomb: A Spinjitzu Master can. A Spinjitzu Master cannot. To move forward, don't look ahead to find his resting spot."

"That's food for thought," Cole said.

"Speaking of food," Jay yelped, "we're about to be some!"

There was a giant octopus on their tail!

"We have to go faster!" Kai said.

"Hold on!" Cole blasted the ship into high gear.

"What kind of weapons does this thing have?" Jay asked.

"We don't need weapons," Zane said, pointing. "Aim for that rock!"

Cole steered their ship through a hole in the giant rock. The octopus followed – but it was too big. It got stuck.

"Way to go, *Rex*! Way to go!" cheered Jay.

A few minutes later, *Rex* floated up into the mouth of the underground tomb, and the ninja scrambled out. Jay spotted a piece of Morro's robes torn on a rock. The Master of Wind was already there!

"There goes any hope Morro couldn't find this place." Jay sighed.

"Hey, stay positive," Kai reminded him. "We're about to risk our lives going through traps, and all we have to rely on is one another. We're lucky we got this far."

THE TOMB OF THE FIRST SPINJITZU MASTER

"The First Spinjitzu Master," Cole said, gazing up at a giant statue. "Creator of all Ninjago."

Suddenly, a computer voice behind them said, "Destination reached. Auto return initiated." *Rex* powered up and disappeared.

"Auto return?" Jay shrieked. "No! Bad *Rex*!"

"Our weapons were in there," Zane said.

Kai sighed. "No sword, no powers, no problem. We can do this, guys. As long as we've got one another."

The ninja made their way down a long hallway. At the end, a stone door opened. Inside a round room, there were sixteen more doors.

"This could be the first test," Cole said.

"We're supposed to pick a door," Kai said. "But which one?"

"What was it Misako said?" Jay asked.

Zane repeated the riddle: "A Spinjitzu Master can. A Spinjitzu Master cannot. To move forward, don't look ahead to find his resting spot."

"A Spinjitzu Master can what?" Kai asked.

"Sixteen doors for sixteen realms?" Jay suggested.

Cole nodded. "Could be. Let me guess: pick the wrong door and we'll be in a realm of hurt."

"We can figure this out," Kai said, focusing. "A Spinjitzu Master can . . . can . . ."

Jay pointed to one of the doors. "The symbol above this door – it's a tornado! 'A Spinjitzu Master can.' This could be the one, right?" He reached for the handle.

"Jay, wait!" Zane shouted. He was getting a message from Pixal. "Step away from that door."

"What is it?" Jay asked.

"We're inside a zoetrope," Zane told him. "The engravings create a moving image when the room spins."

"I don't get it," said Cole.

"A Spinjitzu Master can . . ." Kai blurted. "We need to do Spinjitzu!"

Zane began to turn around and around. *Ninja-go!* As he spun, the sixteen different images blended together to look like one.

"That's the one," Zane said, pointing to a door with a curved symbol. "That's the door out."

"I don't know, Zane," said Cole. "Isn't that the same door we came in by? Are you sure?"

"Do you really want to doubt a Nindroid?" asked Zane.

Kai stepped forward. "Open the door. Let's find out."

Jay pushed the door open, revealing a large cavern. At the far end of the room, a golden staff glowed on a pedestal.

"That wasn't here before," Cole said. "How can this be the way if it's the same way we came in?"

Kai marched forward. "Welcome to the Tomb of the First Spinjitzu Master."

Jay smiled at Zane. "Nice one, Zane. Who needs the Sword of Sanctuary when you've got a Nindroid?"

SPY GAMES

"The staff of the First Spinjitzu Master," Kai said.

"This is the second test," Cole said. "Zane, what do you think?"

Zane scanned his inner computer. "Pixal can see no pattern. For this room, I'm at a loss."

"The first test was 'a Spinjitzu Master CAN'," said Jay. "So this one's 'a Spinjitzu Master CANNOT.' I'm not sure I like the sound of that . . ."

Zane stepped forward. His foot triggered a booby trap. The ninja leapt out of the way as darts flew at them!

"That was a close one," Zane said.

"Every step is a trap," Jay groaned.

"I suspect the golden staff is a lever to deactivate the traps," Zane said. "How does one reach the staff if it becomes more difficult to get there with every step?"

"So if a Spinjitzu Master cannot do it, how are we supposed to reach the staff?" Cole wondered.

Kai raced towards the staff, flipping and spinning through the air. "Watch and learn!"

Kai darted across the room. But every time he got near the staff, he set off more traps. Spikes shot at him. Flames blazed. Rocks swung from the ceiling. "I can make it," Kai grunted.

He kept his eyes on the prize even as pieces of the floor crumbled away. With every step he took, the room became more dangerous. "Okay," Kai finally admitted. "Maybe I can't."

"Will you please stop moving?!" Jay screamed.

"I can make it!" Kai shouted, sure of himself again. "It's just a hop, skip, and a jump." He crouched low to leap towards the staff – but then he slipped. The ground beneath him fell away, and he had to scramble to safety.

"I don't know how much more we can take," Cole said, shaking his head.

"The riddle clearly said this is a test a Spinjitzu Master cannot do," Jay said. "So why aren't we listening to the riddle?"

"Wait!" Cole had an idea. "What if it's a trick? What if the reason we can't do it is because we were never meant to reach the staff? What's the first rule of being a ninja?"

"A ninja never quits," Zane said.

"Exactly," Cole nodded. "That's why we can't do it. Because a ninja would never give up."

"What are you saying?" Kai asked. "We just quit? Are you insane?"

"Trust me," Cole said. Then he jumped into the dark pit below.

"Cole!" Jay, Kai and Zane screamed.

Cole's voice faded away in the darkness. Then he shouted from down below. "Woo-hoo! Come on down and enjoy the ride!"

"He's okay," Zane cheered. He, Kai and Jay all jumped into the blackness. A moment later, the ninja were slipping down a long ice-slide.

"Try to stay together," Kai said.

"Stay *together*?" Jay shrieked. "I'm just trying to stay in one piece!"

THE MAZE

At the bottom, the ninja spilled out into a giant, icy cavern.

"Is everyone okay?" Zane asked.

Kai shook his head. "What did we get ourselves into?"

"It's a maze!" Jay said happily. "I'm great at mazes! The trick with mazes is, if you follow the wall, you'll eventually find your way out. Just don't make any drastic turns."

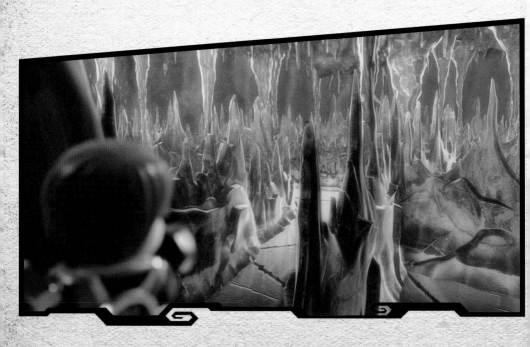

"Whoa," Kai said. He peered into one of the icy walls and saw his own reflection – but he was much older! "The maze is showing us what we'll look like in the future!"

Cole gasped. "Why can't I see my reflection?"

"Probably because you're a ghost," Kai said.

Zane shook his head. "Ghosts cast reflections, Kai. He's just looking in the wrong place."

"I'm looking at the same place you are!" Cole yelped. "So why can you all see yourselves, but I'm completely gone? Am I not going to make it?!"

"Hey, guys," Jay said. "Guess what? In the future, I get an awesome eye patch!"

Cole rubbed at the wall again, trying to see himself. But instead, he saw someone else. A reflection – and then the icy wall shattered.

"It's Morro!" Cole screamed. "He's still in Lloyd's body, and he's in the maze, too!"

"All you ninja do is talk," Morro hissed. "Blah, blah, blah. I'll stop you from talking!"

Morro chased Jay through the maze. He slashed at him with his sword. "He's attacking an unarmed man!" Jay called out.

"We're coming for you!" Kai promised.

Cole, Kai and Zane raced after Morro and Jay. When they caught up, the Master of Wind growled at them. He was strong enough to fight all four ninja at once. Especially when the ninja had no powers or weapons!

Suddenly, Kai had an idea. He'd noticed that every time Morro's sword cut through an ice wall, two more walls grew back in its place.

"Catch me if you can!" Kai said, dashing away.

Morro raced after Kai, slashing his blade at any walls in his way. Dozens of new ones sprouted up around him. Before long, he was trapped in an icy prison of his own making.

"You can't trap me, ninja," Morro yelled. "I'll find you. Just wait, you'll see!"

THE FINAL RIDDLE

"How do we get out of here?" Jay asked.

Cole thought about the riddle again. "To move forward, don't look ahead . . ."

"Don't look ahead." Jay said. "Look below!"

"There's light," Kai said, looking through the icy floor below them. "Everyone, dig!"

Cole, Jay, Kai and Zane dug through the floor and fell into another hidden chamber.

At the bottom, they all stopped. The bones of an ancient ninja lay before them, along with a simple headstone.

"It's him," Kai said, bowing. "The First Spinjitzu Master."

"The Realm Crystal," Zane said. He gently pried the crystal out of the skeleton's hands.

"How does it work?" Kai asked.

Morro's evil laugh rang out overhead. "How it works is . . . you'll hand over the crystal, or say good-bye to your friend!"

Morro had finally left Lloyd's body – and now he had a sword to Lloyd's throat!

"I'm sorry," Lloyd moaned. "I couldn't stop him."

"So what'll it be?" Morro asked. "The crystal or your friend?"

"If we hand him the crystal, he'll curse Ninjago and every other realm," Zane whispered.

"But look at Lloyd – he's too weak to protect himself," Cole said.

"Both options totally stink," Jay muttered.

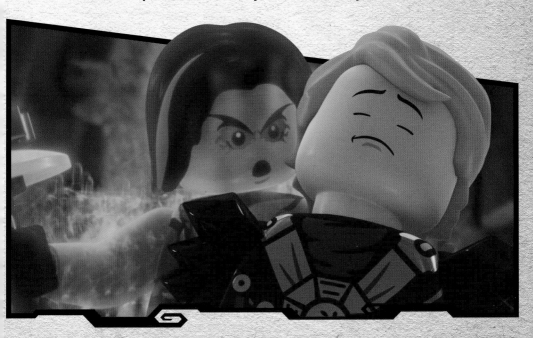

"Give me the Realm Crystal or else!" Morro shouted.

"Our powers," Kai said suddenly. "Now that Morro's out of Lloyd's body, our powers are starting to come back!"

"Yeah, but they're weak," Jay noted. "And we're in no position to fight back now."

Kai clenched his fists, holding the Realm Crystal tight. "Leave that to me . . . Be ready." He yelled up to Morro, "We'll give you the Realm Crystal!"

Kai squeezed the crystal in his hand and threw it. When Morro caught it, it burned him. Kai had used his fire power to heat it up!

With a roar of pain, Morro dropped the crystal . . . straight into the roaring river below. "The crystal!" he howled. Furious, Morro pushed Lloyd into the water.

"Lloyd!" the ninja screamed. The river was dragging Lloyd into raging rapids.

Kai and Cole ran after Lloyd. "But I can't get to him," Kai wailed. "I can't swim!"

"You can't swim?" Cole asked. "I can't touch the water! I'm a ghost, remember?"

While Cole and Kai chased Lloyd, Jay and Zane took on Morro. Zane shot a blast of water at Morro's sword, freezing it solid.

"Nice one, Zane!" Jay called out.

Downriver, Lloyd was getting closer and closer to the rapids. Kai leaped after him!

"Kai's got Lloyd!" Jay yelled. "But who's got Kai?"

Cole reached over the edge. With a mighty tug, he pulled both Kai and Lloyd out just before they plunged into the pit of bubbling lava below.

A moment later, the Realm Crystal sailed over the waterfall.

Suddenly, it slowed and hovered in midair. Then it soared upwards again! Using the power of the wind, Morro pulled the Realm Crystal straight into his own hands. He fled with the stone.

"Get him, everyone!" Cole cried.

But it was too late. Morro was gone – and so was the crystal.

The ninja raced out of the tomb just in time to see Morro disappear. They had failed in their quest to get the crystal.

"You all sacrificed so much to save me," Lloyd said gratefully. "But now Ninjago's going to be cursed."

"But we have you," Zane said, putting his hand on Lloyd's shoulder.

"And our powers are back," Jay said.

"As you get stronger, so will we," Cole vowed. He looked at his brothers and smiled. "They haven't seen us at full strength yet!"